ISBN: 9781088266236

Dedication

To Resa and Reuben
Patience is not just waiting;
it's how we behave while we wait.

Taryn was excited! It was lunchtime and today they were having her favorite: cheese pizza!
She eagerly, but orderly, walked in the line from her classroom to the cafeteria.

Once there, she stood in line and moved along, when able, getting closer to her yummy slice of pizza, and then...

...Sally bumped into her from behind. She had run to catch up to the line and accidentally bumped into Taryn. She did not say sorry.

Taryn felt this was wrong but did not say anything. Instead, she turned back around, to wait for her pizza. But then...Sally stepped out of line, and got back into line, IN FRONT OF TARYN!

"You can't cut in line. I was here first. Please move back where you were, Sally," Taryn said.

"NO! I'm hungry and I want some pizza now!" Sally said.

Taryn was beginning to get angry. "But you can't cut! That's not nice and I was here first! You have to move back Sally!" she said again. Taryn was angry now. She jumped up and hit Sally, and they began to fight! Sally PUSHED Taryn and she fell to the ground!

Ms. Smith ran over and broke up the fight and asked what happened.
"Sally cut in line and then pushed me!" Taryn said.
"Is this true, Sally?" Ms. Smith asked.
Sally was silent.
"Sally it's not nice to lose your manners. What should you say to Taryn?" Ms. Smith continued.

Sally was still upset. "But I'm hungry and I want my pizza now! I don't want to wait!" she said.

Tears streamed down Sally's face. Taryn tried to console Sally. Ms. Smith decided to hold up the line so no one can get pizza until the girls have talked about this.

"Sometimes when my brother and I want to watch different things on TV our Mommy says we each have to wait our turn; my Mommy says that waiting for others shows patience and when we are patient with others, they'll be patient with us," she said.

"That's right, Sally, you will still get your pizza, you just have to wait," Ms. Smith added. "It's also nice manners to say you're sorry; can we try that?"
Sally turned to Taryn. "Ok. I'm sorry. Can we stand in line together and get our pizza?" she said.

Taryn remembered her mother talking about something else: forgiveness. "It's when you give people another chance for losing their manners, or for being mean," Mommy had said.

Taryn decided to forgive Sally for pushing her. "Sure!" Taryn said. "Let's go get our pizza!"

The End!

www.ingramcontent.com/pod-product-compliance
Lightning Source LLC
LaVergne TN
LVHW071640160826
845671LV00047B/334

9781088266236